"LET HIM ASK OF GOD"

"LET HIM ASK OF GOD"

Early Accounts of Joseph Smith's First Vision Retold as a Single Narrative

JOSEPH SMITH JR.
MICHAEL JAMES FITZGERALD

Overdue Books Publishing

First edition (rev. 20200927)

E-book edition:

ISBN-10: 1-887309-47-0

ISBN-13: 978-1-887309-47-9

Print edition:

ISBN-10: 1-887309-48-9;

ISBN-13: 978-1-887309-48-6

Cover: Photograph of a stained-glass window representing the First Vision, displayed in the Adams Woods chapel in Los Angeles, California (1913–1959). Now displayed in the Church History Museum, Salt Lake City, Utah. From Wikimedia Commons. In the public domain.

For
Thomas M. Cieslinski
The Missionary Who First
Shared the First Vision with Me

CONTENTS

Acknowledgments

I am indebted to my lifelong friend Tom Cieslinski who invited me to hear the story of the First Vision when I was a teenager, to Milton V. Backman, Jr. whose 1971 book *Joseph Smith's First Vision: The First Vision in Its Historical Context* launched me on a journey that led to writing this book, and to my good friend Nic Judd for his critical suggestions and insightful review of an early version of this book.

Introduction

In honor of the 200th anniversary of Joseph Smith's well-attested First Vision, I've pieced together its primary, first-person[1] and contemporary, third-person accounts into a single narrative.

This book could be considered a "based on actual events" retelling of the story, or even historical fiction, subjectively written but intended to help create a comprehensive picture of what actually took place on that sprint morning in 1820. It takes as little literary license as possible, though certainly some is required. I did my best to preserve the original accounts with great sensitivity as I wove the parts together, seeking to favor the reader's experience over the critic's.

I modernized or some corrected spelling, added quotation marks, altered some word order and punctuation, dropped a few words and phrases in favor of clarity, and added transition words to help with the flow of the text.

I also rewrote the third person accounts in first person. I reasoned that the secondary, third-person accounts which came from witnesses who actually heard the words fall from Joseph's lips,[2] that I could trust that their accounts were faithful to Joseph's own words.

This is slippery ground for a historian, but not so much for a storyteller. Historians and storytellers both can build faith.

Now a few words on my faith. I first heard the story of the First Vision from a close friend when I was 17 years old and not yet a member of The Church of Jesus Christ of Latter-day Saints. The moment I heard the story, I believed it with all my heart. It filled my soul with fire and light and set me on a lifelong path of faith. Over four decades later, I'm still on the path.

I learned on my journey to baptism that disbelief is based on filling in blanks with assumptions. I call it "closed case" thinking. Real faith, on the other hand, is based on seeking with an open heart and mind. It is "cold case" thinking, a relentless detective's search for answers, never giving up, never stopping short but searching far and wide and digging deep for the whole truth.[3]

When I meet Joseph again and he beats me soundly at stick pull, should he beat me over the head with that stick for being so audacious to publish a book like this, I'll take my lumps.

My testimony, from the beginning of my journey until now, is that Joseph Smith is a prophet of God, the prophet foreordained to open this last dispensation, the dispensation of the fulness of times, and one sent to prepare the world for the Second Coming of Jesus Christ, whose coming is near, "even at the doors."[4]

"I Knew Not Who Was Right or Who Was Wrong"

THE LORD DOES REVEAL himself to me. I know it. He revealed himself to me first when I was a mere boy. I will tell you about it.

When I was a youth about the age of twelve years, I began to think about these things and my mind became seriously impressed with regard to the all-important concerns for the welfare of my immortal soul.

I began seriously to reflect upon the necessity of being prepared for a future state of existence, but how or in what way to prepare myself was a question, as yet, undetermined in my own mind. I perceived that it was a question of infinite importance, and that the salvation of my soul depended upon a correct understanding of the same. I saw that if I understood not the way, it would be impossible to walk in it, except by chance; and the thought of resting my hopes of eternal life upon chance, or blind uncertainties, was more than I could endure.

As I began to reflect upon the importance of being prepared for this future state, and upon enquiring about the plan of salvation, I pondered many things in my heart concerning the situation of the world, of mankind, and the contentions and divisions, the wickedness and abominations, and the darkness which pervaded the minds of mankind.

Being wrought up in my mind respecting the subject of religion and looking at the different systems taught by the children of men, I knew not who was right or who was wrong. And considering it of first importance that I should be right in matters that involved eternal consequences, my mind became exceedingly distressed.

I became convicted of my sins and by searching the scriptures I found that mankind did not come unto the Lord, but had apostatized from the true and living faith. I found there was no society or denomination that built upon the gospel of Jesus Christ as recorded in the New Testament, and I felt to mourn for my own sins and for the sins of the world. And when I considered these things, my heart exclaimed, "Well hath the wise man said, The fool saith in his heart, there is no God."[1]

This led me to searching the scriptures, believing, as I was taught, that they contained the word of God. I learned in the scriptures that God was the same yesterday, today, and forever,[2] that he was no respecter to persons[3] for he was God.

I looked upon the sun, the glorious luminary of the earth, and also the moon, rolling in their majesty through the heavens, and also the stars shining in their courses, and the earth also upon which I stood, and the beast of the field, and the fowls of heaven, and the fish of the waters, and also man walking forth upon the face of the earth in majesty and in the strength of beauty, whose power and intelligence in governing these things are so exceeding great and marvelous, even in the likeness of Him who created them

My heart exclaimed that all these bear testimony and bespeak an Omnipotent and Omnipresent power, a Being who maketh laws and decreeth and bindeth all things in their bounds, who filleth eternity, who was and is and will be from all eternity to all eternity.

When I considered all these things and that that Being seeketh such to worship him as worship Him in spirit and in truth,[4] I then reflected upon the immense number of doctrines now in the world, which had given rise to many hundreds of different denominations. The great question to be decided in my mind, was: "If any one of these denominations be the church of Christ, which one is it?"

"An Unusual Excitement on the Subject of Religion"

❧

SOMETIME IN THE second year after our removal to Manchester, in my fifteenth year, there was in the neighborhood where we lived a reformation among the different religious denominations—an unusual excitement on the subject of religion.

I found that there was a great clash in religious sentiment. It commenced with the Methodists, but soon became general among all the sects in that region of country. Indeed, the whole district seemed affected by it and great multitudes united themselves to the different religious parties, which created no small stir and division among the people, some crying, "Lo here," and some, "Lo there."[1]

If I went to one society, they referred me to one plan, and another to another plan, each one pointing to his own particular creed as the *summum bonum*[2] of perfection. Considering that all could not be right, and that God could not be the author of so much confusion,[3] I determined to investigate the subject more fully, believing that if God had

5

a church, it would not be split up into factions, and that if he taught one society to worship one way, and administer in one set of ordinances, he would not teach another principles which were diametrically opposed.

I discovered the world of religion working under a flood of errors which, by virtue of their contradictory opinions and principles, laid the foundation for the rise of such different sects and denominations whose feelings toward each other all too often were poisoned by hate, contention, resentment, and anger.

Some were contending for the Methodist faith, some for the Presbyterian, and some for the Baptist. But notwithstanding the great love which the converts to these different faiths expressed at the time of their conversion and the great zeal manifested by the respective clergy who were active in getting up and promoting this extraordinary scene of religious feeling in order to have everybody converted, as they were pleased to call it (let them join what sect they pleased), yet when the converts began to file off some to one party and some to another, it was seen that the seemingly good feelings of both the priests and the converts were mere pretense, more pretended than real. For a scene of great confusion and bad feeling ensued: priest contending against priest, and convert against convert, so that all their good feelings one for another (if they ever had any) were entirely lost in a strife of words and a contest about opinions.

In time, my father's family was proselyted to the Presbyterian faith. Four of them joined that church, namely, my mother Lucy, my brothers Hyrum and Samuel Harrison, and my sister Sophronia.

I became serious and was desirous to know what

Church to join, but could not find out which of all the sects were right. Applying myself to these sects, and my intimate acquaintance with those of the different denominations, led me to marvel exceedingly, for I discovered that they did not adorn their profession by a holy walk and godly conversation, agreeable to what I found contained in that sacred depository. This was a grief to my soul. I wanted to get religion too and feel and shout like the rest, but I could feel nothing.

After I had sufficiently convinced myself to my own satisfaction that darkness covered the earth and gross darkness the nations,[4] the hope of ever finding a sect or denomination that was in possession of unadulterated truth left me.

❦

DURING THIS TIME OF GREAT EXCITEMENT MY MIND WAS called up to serious reflection and great uneasiness, but though my feelings were deep and often poignant, still I kept myself aloof from all these parties, though I attended their several meetings as occasion would permit. In process of time my mind became somewhat partial to the Methodist sect, and I felt some desire to be united with them, but so great was the confusion and strife amongst the different denominations that it was impossible for a person young as I was and so unacquainted with men and things to come to any certain conclusion who was right and who was wrong.

My mind at different times was greatly excited, for the cry and tumult were so great and incessant. The Presbyterians were most decided against the Baptists and

Methodists, and used all their powers of either reason or sophistry to prove their errors, or at least to make the people think they were in error. On the other hand, the Baptists and Methodists in their turn were equally zealous in endeavoring to establish their own tenets and disprove all others.

In the midst of this war of words, and tumult of opinions, I often said to myself, "What is to be done? Who of all these parties are right? Or are they all wrong together? And if any one of them be right which is it? And how shall I know it?"

I felt that there was only one truth and that those who understood it correctly would all understand it in the same way. Nature had endowed me with a keen, critical intellect and so I looked through the lens of reason and common sense and with pity and contempt upon those systems of religion, which were so opposed to each other and yet were all obviously based on the scriptures.

Until I could become satisfied in relation to this question, I could not rest contented. To trust to the decisions of fallible man, and build my hopes upon the same without any certainty and knowledge of my own, would not satisfy the anxious desires that pervaded my breast. To decide, without any positive and definite evidence on which I could rely, upon a subject involving the future welfare of my soul, was revolting to my feelings.

"Let Him Ask of God"

THUS WHILE I was laboring under the extreme difficulties caused by the contests of these parties of religionists, the only alternative that seemed to be left was to read the scriptures and endeavor to follow their directions. Accordingly, I began in an attitude of faith my own investigation of the word of God, feeling that it was the best way to arrive at the knowledge of the truth. I commenced perusing the sacred pages of the Bible, with sincerity believing the things that I read.

I had not proceeded very far in this endeavor when my eyes fell upon a particular verse. While thinking of this matter, I one day opened the Bible promiscuously and the first passage that struck me was from the Epistle of James, first chapter and fifth verse, which reads, "If any of you lack wisdom, let him ask of God, that giveth to all men liberally and upbraideth not, and it shall be given him."

My mind caught hold of this verse. Never did any passage of scripture come with more power to the heart of man than this did at this time to mine. It seemed to enter with great force into every feeling of my heart. I reflected on it again and again, knowing that if any person needed wisdom from God, I did. For how to act, I did not know, and unless I could get more wisdom than I then had, I would never know. For the teachers of religion of the different sects understood the same passage of scripture so differently as to destroy all confidence in settling the question by an appeal to the Bible.

From this promise in James, I learned that it was the privilege of all men to ask God for wisdom, with the sure and certain expectation of receiving, liberally, and without being upbraided for so doing. This was cheering information to me, tidings of great joy. It was like a light shining forth in a dark place to guide one to the path in which he should walk.

I now saw that if I inquired of God, there was not only a possibility, but a probability—yea, more, a certainty— that I should obtain a knowledge, which, of all the doctrines, was the doctrine of Christ; and, which, of all the churches, was the church of Christ. I considered this scripture an authorization for me to solemnly call upon my Creator to present my needs before Him with the certain expectation of some success.

Believing the word of God, then, I had confidence in the declaration of James. Information was what I most desired at this time, and with a fixed determination I sought to obtain it.

At length, I came to the conclusion that I must either remain in darkness and confusion or else I must do as James directs, that is, ask of God. I at last came to the determination to ask of God, concluding that if he gave wisdom to them that lacked wisdom, and would give liberally and not upbraid, I might venture.

"I Cried unto the Lord for Mercy"

⚜

SO IN ACCORDANCE with this my determination to ask of God, under a realizing sense that He had said (if the Bible be true), "Ask and you shall receive, knock and it shall be opened, seek and you shall find,"[1] I immediately retired to the woods to make the attempt—to a small, silent grove of trees a short distance from my father's house—where he had a clearing, and I went to the stump where I had stuck my axe when I had quit work.

It was on the morning of a beautiful clear day early in the spring of 1820.[2] It was the first time in my life that I had made such an attempt, for amidst all my anxieties I had never as yet made the attempt to pray vocally.

After I had retired to this secret place where I had previously designed to go, having looked around me and finding myself alone, I kneeled down and began to call upon the Lord in solemn prayer, offering up the desires of my heart to Him, pouring out to the Lord with fervent determination the earnest desires of my soul.

I cried unto the Lord for mercy— for there was none else to whom I could go and obtain mercy—saying, "O Lord, what Church shall I join and which of all the sects is right?"

"Thick Darkness Gathered around Me"

AT FIRST I made a fruitless attempt to pray. I heard a noise behind me, like some person walking towards me. I sprung up on my feet, and looked around, but saw no person or thing that was calculated to produce the noise of walking.

I strove again to pray, but could not for the noise of walking seemed to draw nearer. I had scarcely done so when immediately I wasseized upon by some power which entirely overcame me and had such astonishing influence over me as to bind my tongue so that I could not speak. My tongue seemed to be swollen and cleaved to the roof of my mouth so that I could not utter a word.

The adversary then made several strenuous efforts to cool my ardent soul. I was severely tempted by the powers of darkness which endeavored to overcome me. He filled my mind with doubts and brought to mind all manner of inappropriate images to prevent me from obtaining my object. Thick darkness gathered around me and it seemed to me for a time as if I were doomed to sudden destruction.

Exerting all my powers, I called on the Lord in mighty prayer to deliver me out of the power of this enemy which had seized upon me.As I kneeled again, my mouth was opened, my tongue liberated, and I was enabled to pray in the fervency of spirit and in faith.

"I Was Enwrapped in a Heavenly Vision"

AT THE VERY moment of great alarm, when I was ready to sink into despair and abandon myself to destruction—not to an imaginary ruin, but to the power of some actual being from the unseen world who had such a marvelous power as I had never before felt in any being.

While thus pouring out my soul, anxiously desiring an answer from God, darkness gave way from my mind, and I saw a pillar of fire, , a light, a very bright and glorious light in the heavens above, exactly over my head, above the brightness of the sun. It no sooner appeared than I found myself delivered from the enemy which held me bound.

At first the light seemed to be at a considerable distance. As it drew nearer, it increased in brightness and magnitude, so that by the time it reached the tops of the trees, the whole wilderness for some distance around was illuminated in a most glorious and brilliant manner.

It continued descending, slowly and gradually, until it rested upon the earth, and I was enveloped in the midst of it. When it first fell upon me, it produced at that sacred moment a peculiar sensation throughout my whole system. I was filled with the Spirit of God and with joy unspeakable. The Lord heard my cry in the wilderness and had opened the heavens upon me. I was enwrapped in a heavenly vision.

I expected to have seen the leaves and boughs of the trees consumed as soon as the light came in contact with them; but perceiving that it did not produce that effect, I was encouraged with the hopes of being able to endure its presence.

My mind was caught away from the objects with which I was surrounded, the natural world around me was excluded from my view so that I would be open to the presentation of heavenly and spiritual things.

"This Is My Beloved Son. Hear Him."

❧❀❧

I SAW THE LORD. In the midst of this pillar of flame—which was spread all around and yet nothing consumed—a glorious Personage appeared.[1] He had a light complexion, blue eyes, and a piece of white cloth drawn over his shoulders. His right arm was bare.

He touched my eyes with his finger and said, "Joseph, this is my beloved Son, hear him." As soon as the Lord had touched my eyes with His finger, another Personage came to the side of the first. I immediately saw it was the Savior.

The two Personages who stood above me in the air[2] exactly resembled each other in features, stature, and likeness, and were surrounded with a brilliant light which eclipsed the sun at noonday, with a brightness and glory that defy all description.

The Savior then spoke to me, saying, "Joseph, my son, thy sins are forgiven thee." He told me that my prayers had been answered, that He had decided to grant me a special blessing, and that He was the Son of God.

I was then informed upon the subjects which for some time previously agitated my mind. I addressed this second Person, saying, "O Lord, what church shall I join? Must I join the Methodist church?"

I was answered, "No, they are not my people, they have all gone astray, and there is none that doeth good, no not one."[3] I was told that they were all wrong and I must join none of the sects or denominations, for all were believing in incorrect doctrines and, consequently, none of them was acknowledged of God as his church and kingdom.

The Personage who addressed me also said that all their creeds were an abomination in his sight, that those professors were all corrupt, that the everlasting covenant had been broken,[4] and, "Behold the world lieth in sin at this time. They have turned aside from the gospel and keep not my commandments. They draw near to me to with their lips, but their hearts are far from me. They teach for doctrines the commandments of men, having a form of godliness, but they deny the power thereof."[5]

"Mine anger is kindling against the inhabitants of the earth,[6] to visit them according to their ungodliness,[7] and to bring to pass that which hath been spoken by the mouth of the prophets and apostles. Behold and lo, I come quickly, as it is written of me,[8] in the cloud, clothed in the glory of my Father.[9]

"Go thy way, walk in my statutes and keep my commandments. Behold, I am the Lord of glory. I was crucified for the world that all those who believe on my name may have eternal life."[10]

He again forbade me to join with any of them and I was expressly commanded to "go not after them." At the same time, I was further commanded to wait patiently, receiving a promise that the true doctrine of Christ, and the complete truth and fulness of the gospel, should at some future time be made known unto me.

I saw many angels in this vision and many other things did the Lord say unto me which I cannot write at this time.

"My Soul Was Filled with Love"

✤

AFTER THE VISION WITHDREW, when I came to myself again, I found myself lying on my back, looking up into heaven. I endeavored to arise, but felt uncommonly feeble. It was some time before my strength returned.

When the vision closed, it left my mind in an indescribable state of calmness and peace. My soul was filled with love, and for many days I could rejoice with great joy, for the Lord was with me.

Comforted, I went into the house. And as I leaned up to the fireplace, mother inquired what the matter was. I replied, "Never mind, all is well—I am well enough off." I then said to my mother, "I have learned for myself that Presbyterianism is not true."

"Why Should the Powers of Darkness Combine against Me?"

✧❦✧

W HEN I WENT HOME and told the people that I had a revelation, and that all the churches were corrupt, I could find none that would believe the heavenly vision.

For example, some few days after I had this vision, I happened to be in company with one of the Methodist preachers who was very active in the before mentioned religious excitement, and conversing with him on the subject of religion, I took occasion to give him an account of the vision which I had had. I was greatly surprised at his behavior. He treated my communication not only lightly, but with great contempt, saying it was all of the devil, that there was no such thing as visions or revelations in these days, that all such things had ceased with the apostles and that there never would be any more of them.

I soon found that my telling the story had excited a great deal of prejudice against me among professors of religion and was the cause of great persecution which continued to increase. They persecuted me, and they have persecuted me ever since. And though I was an obscure boy only between fourteen and fifteen years of age and my circumstances in life such as to make a boy of no consequence in the world, yet men of high standing would take notice sufficiently to excite the public mind against me and create a hot persecution, and this was common among all the sects: all united to persecute me.

It seems as though the adversary was aware, at a very early period of my life, that I was destined to prove a disturber and an annoyer of his kingdom; else why should the powers of darkness combine against me? Why the opposition and persecution that arose against me, almost in my infancy?

I have pondered these things in my heart and it often caused me serious reflection, both then and since, how very strange it was that an obscure boy of a little over fourteen years of age, and one too who was doomed to the necessity of obtaining a scanty maintenance by his daily labor, should be thought a character of sufficient importance to attract the attention of the great ones of the most popular sects of the day so as to create in them a spirit of the bitterest persecution and reviling.

They thought to put me down, but they haven't succeeded, and they can't do it. When I have proved that I am right, and get all the world subdued under me, I think I shall deserve something.

But strange or not, so it was, and was often cause of great sorrow to myself.

It was nevertheless a fact, that I had had a vision. I have thought since that I felt much like as Paul did when he made his defense before King Agrippa and related the account of the vision he had, when he saw a light and heard a voice, but still there were but few who believed him.

Some said he was dishonest, others said he was mad, and he was ridiculed and reviled, but all this did not destroy the reality of his vision.

He had seen a vision. He knew he had, and all the persecution under heaven could not make it otherwise, and though they should persecute him unto death, yet he knew, and would know to his latest breath, that he had both seen a light and heard a voice speaking unto him, and all the world could not make him think or believe otherwise.

So it was with me. I had actually seen a light and in the midst of that light, I saw two Personages, and they did in reality speak to me, or one of them did, and though I was hated and persecuted for saying that I had seen a vision, yet it was true, and while they were persecuting me, reviling me, and speaking all manner of evil against me, falsely, for so saying, I was led to say in my heart, "Why persecute me for telling the truth?" I have actually seen a vision, "and who am I that I can withstand God?"[1] Or why does the world think to make me deny what I have actually seen? For I had seen a vision, I knew it, and I knew that God knew it, and I could not deny it, neither dare I do it, at least I knew that by so doing, I would offend God and come under condemnation.

I had now got my mind satisfied so far as the sectarian world was concerned, that it was not my duty to join with any of them, but continue as I was until further directed, for I had found the testimony of James to be true, that a man who lacked wisdom might ask of God, and obtain, and not be upbraided.[2]

Appendix

Here are the sources for this book and some additional resources for further study.

Primary First-Person Accounts

1. Joseph Smith History, circa Summer 1832, 1–3. See https://www.josephsmithpapers.org/paper-summary/history-circa-summer-1832/1. Accessed March 2020.
2. Joseph Smith Journal, November 9–11, 1835, 23–24. See https://www.josephsmithpapers.org/paperSummary/journal-1835-1836?p=24. Accessed March 2020.
3. Joseph Smith Journal, November 9, 1835, 120–121. Repurposed and edited by Warren Parrish. See https://www.josephsmithpapers.org/paperSummary/history-1834-1836?p=124. Accessed March 2020.

4. Joseph Smith History, 1838–1856, volume A-1, 2–3. See https://www.josephsmithpapers.org/paperSummary/history-circa-june-1839-circa-1841-draft-2?p=2. See also Joseph Smith–History 1:1–26. See https://www.churchofjesuschrist.org/study/scriptures/pgp/js-h/1.1-26?lang=eng#primary.

5. Joseph Smith History, 1838–circa 1841, draft copy, 2–4. Howard Coray's edited copy of the 1838 account. See https://www.josephsmithpapers.org/paperSummary/history-circa-1841-draft-draft-3?p=2. Accessed March 2020.

6. Joseph Smith History, circa 1841, fair copy, 2–4. Howard Coray's fair copy of the 1838 account. See https://www.josephsmithpapers.org/paperSummary/history-circa-1841-fair-copy?p=2. Accessed March 2020.

7. Joseph Smith, "Church History," *Times and Seasons,* March 1, 1842. 3:706–707. Popularly known as the "Wentworth Letter." See https://www.josephsmithpapers.org/paperSummary/church-history-1-march-1842?p=1. See also https://archive.org/details/TimesAndSeasonsVol3/page/n199/mode/2up. Accessed March 2020.

8. Israel Daniel Rupp, *He Pasa Ekklesia: An Original History of the Religious Denominations at Present Existing in the United States*, 1844, 404–405. Word-for-word copy of Joseph Smith's 1842 account also known as the Wentworth Letter. See https://www.josephsmithpapers.org/

paperSummary/latter-day-saints-1844?p=1. See
also https://archive.org/details/
hepasaekklesiaaooruppgoog/page/n414/
mode/2up. Accessed March 2020.

Secondary First-Person Account

1. David Nye White, "The Prairies, Joe Smith, the
   Temple, the Mormons, &c.," *Pittsburgh Weekly
   Gazette*, September 15, 1843, 3. White
   interviewed Joseph Smith while visiting Nauvoo
   and reported Joseph's account in first person.

Contemporary Third-Person Accounts

1. Orson Pratt, *A[n] Interesting Account of Several
   Remarkable Visions and of the Late Discovery of
   Ancient American Records*, 1840, 3–5. Pamphlet
   published in Edinburgh, Scotland containing the
   first published account of the First Vision in
   English. See https://www.josephsmithpapers.org/
   paperSummary/appendix-orson-pratt-an-
   interesting-account-of-several-remarkable-
   visions-1840?p=3. Accessed March 2020.
2. Orson Hyde, *Ein Ruf aus der Wüste: Eine Stimme
   aus dem Schoose [Schosse] der Erde* [A Cry out of
   the Wilderness (Desert): a Voice from the
   Bowels (Bosom) of the Earth], 1842, 14–16.
   Pamphlet published in Frankfurt, Germany
   containing the first non-English publication of

an account of the First Vision. See https://www.
josephsmithpapers.org/paperSummary/orson-
hyde-ein-ruf-aus-der-wste-1842-extract?p=3
(original German) and https://www.
josephsmithpapers.org/paperSummary/orson-
hyde-ein-ruf-aus-der-wste-a-cry-out-of-the-
wilderness-1842-extract-english-translation
(English translation of the German). Accessed
March 2020.

3. Levi Richards, Journal, June 11, 1843. Richards
   wrote this account after hearing Joseph speak
   about his First Vision in a public meeting in
   Nauvoo. See https://www.josephsmithpapers.
   org/paperSummary/levi-richards-journal-11-june-
   1843-extract.

4. Alexander Neibaur, Journal, May 24, 1844, 23–24.
   See https://www.josephsmithpapers.org/
   paperSummary/alexander-neibaur-journal-24-
   may-1844-extract. Accessed March 2020.

5. Charles L. Walker, *Diary of Charles Lowell Walker*,
   (Larson and Larson) 2: 755–756. Available on
   FairMormon.org. Accessed March 2020.

Selected Books

- Milton V. Backman, Jr. *Joseph Smith's First Vision:
  The First Vision in Its Historical Context* (Salt Lake
  City: Bookcraft, 1971).
- Matthew B. Christensen, *The First Vision: A
  Harmonization of Ten Accounts from the Sacred
  Grove* (Springville, Utah: Cedar Fort, 2014).

Note: I was not aware of the content Matthew Christensen's book before I started writing this book. I have not read his book.

- Steven C. Harper, *Joseph Smith's First Vision: A Guide to the Historical Accounts* (Salt Lake City: Deseret Book, 2012).
- Steven C. Harper, *First Vision: Memory and Mormon Origins* (Oxford, England: Oxford University Press, 2019).
- Kerry Muhlestein, *"I Saw the Lord": Joseph's First Vision Combined from Nine Accounts* (Salt Lake City: Deseret, 2020).

Other Resources

- The Church of Jesus Christ of Latter-day Saints, *Ask of God: Joseph Smith's First Vision.* See https://www.youtube.com/watch?v=RBvk_6_dW6k.
- BYU Religious Education, *Joseph Smith's First Vision: Sacred Grove in Palmyra, New York.* See https://www.youtube.com/watch?v=uhzzCPezmRQ.
- Truman G. Madsen, "Joseph Smith Lecture 1: The First Vision and Its Aftermath," BYU Education Week, August 22, 1978. See https://speeches.byu.edu/talks/truman-g-madsen/joseph-smith-first-vision-its-aftermath/. See also https://www.youtube.com/watch?v=ea2v84iPrRM.
- John C. Lefgren and John P. Pratt independently postulated that the date of the First Vision was

Sunday, March 26, 1820. See https://
march26th1820.com/. See also https://
youtu.be/H6MsQ6QBMMY.

- Elena Castro, "The First Vision: A Narrative
from Joseph Smith's Accounts,"
StevenCraigHarper.com, January 14, 2020. See
https://stevencraigharper.com/the-first-vision-a-
narrative-from-joseph-smiths-accounts/.
Accessed March 2020.

Notes

Introduction

1. I count David Nye White's account as a first-person account though it is considered a secondary account.
2. In the case of Charles L. Walker, he heard the account directly from John Alger who heard the story as a small boy from Joseph Smith in Kirtland, Ohio.
3. See Steven C. Harper's *Joseph Smith's First Vision: A Guide to the Historical Accounts* chapters 1 and 8 for an inspiring comparison of seeker versus assumer. I highly recommend his book.
4. Matthew 24:33; Joseph Smith—Matthew 1:39; Doctrine and Covenants 110:16.

1. "I Knew Not Who Was Right or Who Was Wrong"

1. Psalms 14:1.
2. Hebrews 13:8.
3. Acts 10:34.
4. John 4:24.

2. "An Unusual Excitement on the Subject of Religion"

1. Luke 17:21.
2. Latin phrase meaning "the supreme good from which all others are derived" according to Merriam-Webster.
3. 1 Corinthians 14:33.
4. Isaiah 60:2.

4. "I Cried unto the Lord for Mercy"

1. Matthew 7:7.
2. John C. Lefgren and John P. Pratt independently arrived at the date of Sunday, March 26, 1820 as the date of the First Vision. Their evidence is compelling. See "Other Resources" in the appendix.

7. "This Is My Beloved Son. Hear Him."

1. Doctrine and Covenants 84:20–22; Moses 1:1–5.
2. Genesis 32:30; Exodus 24:9–11; Numbers 12:5; Acts 7:55–56; Revelation 4:2–3; 1 Nephi 1:8; Doctrine and Covenants 76:23; Abraham 2:6; 3:11;
3. Psalms 53:3.
4. Isaiah 24:5; Doctrine and Covenants 1:15.
5. Isaiah 29:13; Matthew 15:8–9; Mark 7:6–7.
6. Doctrine and Covenants 1:13.
7. Jude 1:15.
8. Hebrews 10:7.
9. Joseph Smith Translation, Revelation 1:7.
10. Doctrine and Covenants 35:2.

9. "Why Should the Powers of Darkness Combine against Me?"

1. Acts 11:17.
2. James 1:5.

Also By Michael James Fitzgerald

In the Last Day: A Brief Guide to Christ's Second Coming for Latter-day Saints—Revised and Expanded

Behold the Man: A Biblical Narrative of the Last Days of Jesus Christ

The Law of Attraction and the Scriptures: A Guide for Latter-day Saints

www.ingramcontent.com/pod-product-compliance
Lightning Source LLC
Chambersburg PA
CBHW030305030426
42337CB00012B/593